M000200442

"Being true to ourselves is sometimes one of the most difficult challenges in life. This easy to read, interactive book helps open our hearts and minds to truths we may have overlooked and helps propel us to a place of wholeness."

Dr. Thelma Wells (Mama T), CEO, That A Girl and Friends Speakers Agency and That A Girl Enrichment Tours, Author and Speaker

"You will laugh, and you will cry as you read *Moving from Broken to Beautiful.* Yvonne Ortega will become your friend as you discover you're not alone in your life journey. Her honesty, transparency, humor, and uplifting message will fill you with hope that you too can overcome life's challenges and live a full life."

Glenna Salsbury, CSP, CPAE Speaker Hall of Fame
2005 Recipient of Cavett Award
Author, *The Art of the Fresh Start*

"*Moving from Broken to Beautiful* is a must read for ANYONE who is hurting—has ever been hurt—or knows someone who has. I read it nonstop cover to cover! This book and Yvonne's sage professional advice, personal stories, and loving suggestions will serve all who read it. It offers a genuine sense of hope with action steps and journaling areas for self-processing and inner healing."

Sheryl Roush, Author, *Heart of a Woman* and *Heart of a Mother*,
CEO, Sparkle Presentations, Inc.

"I highly recommend Yvonne's book for those seeking strength and comfort and the wisdom to get through their life challenges. You'll be amazed at her story. You'll see how she has been through overwhelming obstacles in her life and come out kicking. Yvonne is the perfect person to help you get through the fear and come out strong, because she has been there and done it herself. You'll love her fresh honesty and eagerness to live life on her terms. I think everyone should read this book. My life is better because I know Yvonne. Do yourself a favor and get to know her too."

Kelly Swanson, Motivational Speaker, Comedienne

"In one small but powerful package, *Moving from Broken to Beautiful* combines the wisdom of an older sister, the straight talk of a counselor, and the unconditional love of a longtime best friend. Author, speaker, and Licensed Professional

Counselor Yvonne Ortega has the professional credentials and personal experience to speak into readers' lives with grace, humor, and genuine caring. Take time to process and interact with each of the book's nine life lessons, and you'll find yourself leaving destructive patterns of thought and behavior as you move toward a life set free by truth. Excellent read!"

Marti Pieper, Author, Collaborative Writer, Editor

"*Moving From Broken to Beautiful* will bring life back to the lifeless, direction to the lost, and beauty to the broken. Read this magnificent book and usher in your healing."

Lisa Jimenez, M.Ed., Author, *Conquer Fear*

"The careful reader of this celebration of real life will see that surviving domestic violence, divorce, death of an only child, and breast cancer are not prerequisites for moving from broken to beautiful, but simply living in a fallen world is. She will find herself lifted up from those universal dark corners in which we've all been stuck, with courage to find that better place God has designed for her. With the honesty and transparency we have come to expect from Yvonne Ortega, she uses her real-life narrative to give her readers permission to say, "Ouch!"

when they are struck, to cry when they hurt, and to reach up when they feel least like doing so."

Sherry Boykin, Author, *Tired of Squeezing a Size 12 "But" into a Size 5 Faith*?

"As a Stephen Minister, Leader and trainer, I love the lessons, affirmations, and scriptural references in Yvonne Ortega's new book. I use this book as I work with people who are suffering, and I highly recommend it to other Stephen Ministers. Thank you, Yvonne, for this wonderful guide for the broken as they move forward in their beautiful lives."

Pam Rambo, Ed.D., Rambo Research and Consulting

"In *Moving from Broken to Beautiful*, Yvonne Ortega has not only provided a guide to healing but has shared her powerful story. As she shares with the readers the lessons learned from her experiences, she also is a companion to the readers as they progress through their own journey. This is a must read for anyone who is facing adversity and ready to travel a path to healing."

Angela L. Edwards, CEO, Castle Thunder Consulting

"Once I started reading *Moving from Broken to Beautiful*, I could not stop until I had finished reading every page. The author has a genuine love ministry for hurting, broken people. Each chapter is flooded with hope for a new life filled with real and permanent success."

Laura Seibert, President of Tidewater Advanced Toastmasters

"I highly recommend *Moving From Broken to Beautiful* for every woman who hurts. Whether you are suffering from cancer, abuse, or loss, Yvonne gently offers to take your hand as you journey toward hope and healing. Courageously sharing from her own story, Yvonne will inspire you to leave fear behind and step forward in faith. Her authenticity, practicality and sense of humor will delight you!"

Becky Harling, Speaker, Author, *Rewriting Your Emotional Script* and *The 30 Day Praise Challenge*

"In *Moving from Broken to Beautiful*, Yvonne Ortega has outlined a way any woman can reconstruct her life. By sharing painful events and emotions from her experience, Yvonne leads the way to healing. This is an ideal book to be used individually or in a group, so women can help each other become as beautiful as God intended them to be. Let's walk this path together."

Debbie Hardy, Author, *Free to Be Fabulous: 100 Ways to Look and Feel Younger from 40, 50, and Beyond*

Moving from Broken to Beautiful:

9 Life Lessons to Help You Move Forward

By Yvonne Ortega

Crystal Pointe Media, Inc. San Diego, CA

Moving from Broken to Beautiful:
9 Life Lessons to Help You Move Forward

© 2015 by Yvonne Ortega

Published by Crystal Pointe Media, Inc.
San Diego, CA

Printed in the United States of America

ISBN-13: 978-0692422182
ISBN-10: 0692422188

Disclaimer

Neither the author nor the publisher is engaged in rendering medical, health, or any other kind of personal professional services in this book. Before embarking on any therapeutic regimen, it is absolutely essential that readers consult with and obtain the approval of their personal health professional before adopting any of the suggestions or drawing inferences from the text. The author and the publisher specifically disclaim all responsibility for any liability, loss, or risk, personal or otherwise, which is incurred as a consequence, directly or indirectly, of the use of and/or application of any of the contents of this book. Some names and identifying details have been changed to protect the privacy of individuals.

In loving memory of my mother,

Carlotta Ortega,

A woman who moved from broken to beautiful.

Also in loving memory of my son,

Brian,

his journey ended at a tender age.

Contents

Acknowledgments

Many people helped me along the way. I appreciate all of them.

Sherry Boykin, Liz Garrett, Donna Ortega, Sandra Sessoms-Penny, Ed.D., CPC, Karen Schlender, Nichole Smith, and Renee West gave me their input.

My international online writers group— Geneva Iijima and Wendy Marshall—critiqued my project from start to finish.

Glenna Salsbury, CSP, CPAE, encouraged me to share my message of hope at her Authentic You Retreat, which I attended twice.

Lisa Jimenez, M.Ed., one of my coaches for nine months, held me accountable through the first five chapters and the first Moving from Broken to Beautiful Conference.

Kelly Swanson and Linda Larsen, CSP, held me accountable to complete the life lessons and present the keynote, Moving from Broken to Beautiful, at their Standing Ovation! Keynote Boot Camp.

Sheryl Roush, an Accredited Speaker and my speaking coach, convinced me not to take on more than I could handle. I wouldn't have finished without her.

Numerous Toastmasters clubs allowed me to present sections from the book chapters at their meetings.

Nanette Snipes with FaithWorks Editorial Services edited my book.

The staff at Crystal Pointe Media, Inc. guided me in the process from manuscript to published book and e-book.

My friends in the Advanced Writers and Speakers Association (AWSA), the Christian Communicators, and my church prayed for me.

My father has supported all my endeavors in education, speaking and writing. Thank you, Dad.

And finally, dear readers, thank you for reading this book.

Introduction

As a child, I liked to play school. I gathered the neighborhood kids to be my students. Of course, I was the teacher. I enjoyed school and a weekly visit to the public library. When I held a book in my hands, the smell of that book and the words on the pages delighted me. Music spoke to my soul, and my family listened to me practice piano lessons daily for eight years. Later, I took two more years of piano lessons on my own.

In that world of classes, books, and music, I never dreamed what troubles lay ahead. My parents remained married until Mama passed away. Surely my marriage would also be "until death do [us] part." It ended before death. I exercised and ate right most of the time. How could I receive a diagnosis of a life-threatening illness? I still did. Parents die before their children. That's the natural order. Right? To my dismay, my child passed away first. I'm a defensive driver. Shouldn't that guarantee my safety on the roads? Unfortunately, it didn't.

I learned I live in an imperfect world with imperfect people, and I have an imperfect body. I became philosophical and searched for the meaning of my trials. The deciding moment came when I understood either I could die physically or emotionally, or I could live life to the fullest. To my joy, I realized good could come from every one of those trials.

Perhaps you've been through the death of a loved one, a major move, or the loss of a job, a car, or a home. Maybe you've suffered from a life-threatening illness, sexual assault, or domestic violence. Perhaps you have a special needs child or elderly parents you care for.

If you're like me when you suffer, you wonder why. You might look for physical or spiritual reasons for the struggles. When you go through trials, you want them to end and the sooner the better. I understand. I don't like pain and suffering either. I'll never say, "Bring on the heartache." Enough heartache will come without asking for it.

Any one of the crises I've mentioned above can leave you broken. I wish an easy way existed to learn life lessons without the trauma. I would patent it and sell it at a discount to the first one hundred buyers. Sadly, none exists.

The good news is you can move from broken to beautiful. Perhaps like me, you've become philosophical and searched for the meaning of your trials. You've wondered if good could come from them. In this book, *Moving from Broken to Beautiful*, you will learn nine life lessons to help you move forward.

In each chapter, you will find a life lesson with an accompanying story or two. As you read the story, think of how it applies to you.

At the end of each chapter, you will find three activities. Perhaps you and a friend can do the activities together and thus encourage and support each other. If you have children of a suitable age, maybe you can work on the activities together.

After the activities, you will find three affirmations. Repeat them throughout the day. Write them on sticky notes to place on a kitchen cupboard, your bathroom mirror, the dash of your car, or your desk. Use the affirmations as a screen saver on your computer.

Following the affirmations, you will have a scriptural reading and a prayer. Write the readings on ruled index cards to carry in your pocket or purse. Memorize and meditate on the readings. Discuss the readings with a friend or coworker.

The prayer is for your personal quiet time. You may wish to pray it with your children, a friend, a coworker, or by yourself.

Each chapter ends with a journal page. Pour out your thoughts, emotions, heartaches, and victories on your journal page.

You can purchase a doodle pad to draw pictures of the life lessons and how they apply to you. Your children may enjoy drawing also.

At the end of the book, you will find three appendices. The first one is a list of additional affirmations to help you embrace each life lesson. The second appendix is a list of additional readings. Those readings will help you tie in the life lessons to your spiritual, physical, and emotional life.

If you are musically inclined, you might

set the affirmations or the readings to music.

Perhaps you have drama talents. You can write skits to go with the affirmations or the readings. Your children or friends might enjoy joining you in those creative endeavors.

The third appendix is a list of resources to help you move forward. It provides the links for such support groups as The Compassionate Friends and AA. You may find it helpful to look into the ones that apply to your circumstances.

Thank you for joining me on this journey. My prayer is that you move forward with hope as you apply the nine life lessons to your own life. These lessons first worked for me, and later, for others. I encourage you to give them a chance to work for you.

You may have family members or friends who express a desire to understand your journey in moving from broken to beautiful. Share this book with them or encourage them to buy their own copy.

Coworkers or neighbors may want to help you. Invite them to join you in learning and moving forward by applying the nine life lessons.

Take a copy of this book to your public library or to your church library. Then others can move forward too.

Once again, I encourage you to give these life lessons a chance to work for you. Here's to your new, beautiful life.

Chapter 1: You Can't Change the Past

The first life lesson is that you can't change the past. I went through a painful divorce more than ten years ago. As much as I would like to wipe my ex-husband out of my life's story, I can't. He's part of the story—the good, the bad, and the ugly. And while painful, I have to acknowledge his existence.

Recently I had to update the medical information form at the opthalmologist's office. One of the questions asked about marital status. You'd think one of the choices would be "single again" instead of "divorced." However, whether you call yourself single again or divorced, you can't change the past. You were once married to someone whether the marriage lasted a short time or a long one. I met Marge, a single again woman, at a dinner party. She had been married a long time, but she was still bitter years later.

At the dinner party, Marge talked the entire time about how terrible her former husband was while they were married. He showed up in the first words out of her mouth and dominated the entire conversation. He showed up in every course of the meal—even dessert. I'm pretty sure I saw his face on the chocolate icing of my chocolate cake. It was a never-ending story line. And the more she talked, the more the veins on her forehead popped out. She was still talking about him in the parking lot, and she was probably still talking about him in bed that night to a cat that sat perched at her feet wearing a tired expression. She was probably the reason people came up with the term basket case. I asked her how long they had been divorced. She said, "Twenty years."

He may have made her life miserable once. But the last ten or fifteen years, that misery was her fault.

I hear women say, "If only I hadn't married that jerk, I wouldn't have wasted the best years of my life. If only I hadn't had children with him, I wouldn't need to have contact with him anymore. One of the kids looks just like him. Now I have a daily reminder of him. I wish the kid looked like me."

This is a waste of your time and energy and works against you instead of for you. Stop letting your thoughts focus on the past. Set your eyes on the present and the future.

Maybe you feel as agitated as the woman who divorced her husband twenty years ago. No matter how many times you retell the story of how he wronged you, you remain embroiled in emotional turmoil. The intensity of your rage stays as high as it was the day of your appointment with the divorce lawyer.

Maybe you feel the way other women do. You can repeat, "If only . . ." a thousand times a day, but you can't change the past. No matter how many times you go over your story, you can't undo it. Can you go a day without puking about the past? Remember you can only change the present and the future.

My divorce lawyer once said, "Yvonne, you can't change the past, but you can make a bucket list of one hundred goals."

Within a few days of my lawyer's suggestion, my friend, Penny, told me the same thing. I said, "This is the second time in less than a week someone mentioned a bucket list to me. I'm going to make one."

One of the items on my bucket list was a two-week trip to Alaska by deluxe motor coach, luxury train, and cruise ship. Another one was a trip to Germany. I had read about Alaska and Germany, and they fascinated me. Thanks to the encouragement of my divorce lawyer and my friend, years later I made those trips. I also wanted to clean out my file cabinet, my clothes closet, and my bookcase. It took a week to clean out my file cabinet, another week to clean out my clothes closet, and a third week to clean out my bookcase. I added to the success of recycling and the inventory of the local thrift stores after those three cleanup jobs. When I completed everything on my bucket list, I made a new one.

A former client once told me, "I finally understand that I can't change the past. I have two children who need my time and energy." She stopped, took in a deep breath, and said, "I can't waste my time on 'ancient history' as you call it, Ms. Yvonne. I'm moving forward."

I'm happy to say she did just that.

You can't change the past either. You can change your attitude and make the present and the future the best years of your life.

Life Lesson One Activities:
- Journal about the present and the future.
- Make a bucket list.
- Make a vision board* of your fabulous future.

Life Lesson One Affirmations:
- I can't change the past, but I can change the present and the future.
- Every day I do something to improve my present and my future.
- I'm excited about my future.

*A vision board is a concrete visualization of what you plan for your future. Some people refer to it as an inspiration board or a dream board. You can cut out pictures and words from magazines to depict your future. You can also use computer graphics. Perhaps you draw well and would prefer to do your own artwork. That's fine too. The important thing is to have a vision of your fabulous future. Paste, glue, or tape your pictures and words to a poster board. You now have a collage to inspire you each day to move forward.

Life Lesson One Reading and Prayer:

- "You, Lord, keep my lamp burning; my God turns my darkness into light" (Psalm 18:28).
- "Though you have made me see troubles, many and bitter, you will restore my life again; from the depths of the earth you will bring me up. You will increase my honor and comfort me once more" (Psalm 71:20–21).
- "Finally, brothers and sisters, whatever is true, whatever is noble, whatever is right, whatever is pure, whatever is lovely, whatever is admirable—if anything is excellent or praiseworthy—think about such things" (Philippians 4:8).

Dear God, I've gone over my past so many times I'm sick of hearing myself talk about it.
Help me accept the fact I can't change the past.
Help me think about excellent or praiseworthy things, such as friends or nature.
Amen.

Life Lesson One Journal

Date: _____

Sample Entry: I want a better life. Somehow I will move forward.

_____

_____

_____

_____

_____

_____

_____

_____

_____

_____

_____

_____

_____

_____

_____

_____

_____

_____

_____

_____

_____

_____

_____

_____

_____

Chapter 2: A Bully Can't Beat You in Your Life Journey

The second life lesson in moving from broken to beautiful is that a bully can't beat you in your life journey. My life has had some bullies in it. You know the feeling. All of us face bullies in life at some time either at home or at work. While we each face a different bully, the truth remains the same: a bully can't beat you unless you let him.

An abusive man is a bully. However, he can't mistreat you unless you let him. He can't call you filthy names, curse at you, threaten you, humiliate you, and hurt you unless you let him. I was married to an abusive man. He abused me verbally, emotionally, financially, and physically.

The day I woke up to my worth as a human being and the worth of my child as a precious gift from God, I stood up to my husband. I filed for divorce. Strange how the man who screamed, cursed, and belittled our son and me, suddenly knew how to behave. The threats and abuse stopped. He was probably afraid I, a petite woman barely five feet tall, would call the police again, and my lawyer would have further proof of his unacceptable behavior. He was probably also afraid the legal problems and an arrest could cause him to lose his job, his benefits, and his retirement.

When he didn't comply with the court order to pay alimony and child support, my lawyer said, "Yvonne, call your husband and remind him."

We had already been to court because of his noncompliance. I laughed and said, "If he won't listen to the judge, what makes you think he'll listen to me?"

I sent a letter to his boss. My estranged husband paid the six months of back pay real fast.

Another time in acting like a bully, he called me at my job and said, "You need to come to my office and pick up the check for alimony and child support because you're supposed to have it on the first of the month."

I said, "It's your responsibility to see that I have it on the first of the month." Without another word, I hung up. I told my office secretary never to let a call from him come through again.

She replied, "He said it was an emergency."

"It wasn't an emergency. Anytime he wants to get his own way, he claims it's an emergency." He never called me at work again.

He drove the half hour to the city where I live and left the check to be delivered to my post office mailbox that day.

I also took him back to court and had direct payment set up through his employer. I wouldn't tolerate any more nonsense.

A woman at one of my conferences cried as she told me about the bully in her life. She gathered the strength to separate from him and cherished the peace and quiet in her new apartment. She had separated from him at least six times in the past. He went there crying after each separation. He would say, "I'm sorry. I'll never hurt you again. I'll never cuss at you or call you names again. I've changed. You'll see."

The woman said, "Yvonne, every time I went back to him he reverted to his bullying and became worse. His tears and promises meant nothing."

A year later that woman sent me a brief message and said, "I didn't go back. I realized he would kill me or I would kill him in self-defense. I moved out of state. I finally believe he can't beat me in my life journey."

A bully will be one as long as you cower. Change the game plan. Take charge of your life. Enlist the help of a lawyer, a counselor, and a local domestic violence shelter to take charge of your life. Take your power back and exercise it. You'll love it when he stops bullying you. He may have attacked you physically in the past, but a bully can't beat you in your life journey.

Life Lesson Two Activities:

- Journal about specific steps you can take to keep a bully from beating you in your life journey.
- Journal or draw pictures about what your life will be like without verbal, emotional, and physical abuse.
- Develop a new hobby or interest.

Life Lesson Two Affirmations:

- I'm wise enough to beat a bully.
- I'm confident a bully can't beat me in my life journey.
- I can change the game plan.

Life Lesson Two Reading and Prayer:

- "A hot-tempered person must pay the penalty; rescue them, and you will have to do it again" (Proverbs 19:19).
- "I sought the LORD, and he answered me; he delivered me from all my fears" (Psalm 34:4).
- "I can do all this through him [Christ] who gives me strength" (Philippians 4:13).

*Dear God, fill me with
wisdom and confidence.
I'm tired of being a punching bag
for that bully's mouth and fist.
Give me strength to change
the game plan
for the children's sake and mine.
Amen.*

Life Lesson Two Journal

Date: _____

_____

_____

_____

_____

_____

_____

_____

_____

_____

_____

Chapter 3: You Can't Move from Broken to Beautiful Overnight

When our son graduated from the Navy boot camp, I flew to see him and attend the graduation events. His father was furious because I showed up. He reproached our son for not telling him I would be there. My son felt caught in the middle and asked me not to attend the reception, the last of the graduation events. He didn't want any trouble. His father and stepmother attended the reception. I stayed away from it.

Later, I was upset with myself for not standing up for my parental right to attend my own son's reception. After all, I took time off from work, flew out of state for his boot camp graduation, rented a car, and stayed in a hotel. His father and I were both adults and should have been happy to be there to support and encourage our son.

Fast-forward thirteen years later. Our only child passed away unexpectedly following surgery. My ex-husband said on the phone, "You don't have to come to California for his Celebration of Life service. You can have your own service in Virginia."

This time I didn't cower. I said, "I'm his mother, and I will be there." I also told him I wanted to give a eulogy.

He said, "His girlfriend and his boss are

giving one."

I said, "It's my right as his mother to give a eulogy. It's your right, too, as his father."

To make sure the director of bereavement services knew I existed, I called the church and asked to speak with her. I informed her that I was Brian's mother, and I would be in California for the service. I would also give a eulogy.

I told my ex-husband, "I've hired a professional videographer to make a DVD for the Celebration of Life service. I selected pictures from Brian's infancy to the present."

He said, "His girlfriend is making one."

Once again, I didn't back down and said, "Good, the more the merrier." In another phone call, he and I discussed our desire to create an upbeat mood for the DVD through the pictures and the music.

When I arrived in California, I stayed with a friend who subscribed to the local newspaper. Imagine my gut-wrenching pain when I saw the obituary my ex-husband wrote about our son. He listed himself and his second wife as the parents. Further down in the obituary, he listed me as the birth mother. I gasped and told my friend, "That makes me look like a surrogate mother or a woman who had a child out of wedlock."

After a flood of tears and deep pain, I remembered that our son once said, "Mom, Dad makes me call her (his stepmother) Mom."

At the Celebration of Life service, I made sure to mention my ex-husband's name in the eulogy more than once as my husband and part of the family until our divorce.

What happened between our son's graduation from boot camp and his passing away thirteen years later? How did I change from the fearful people pleaser to an adult woman who would stand up for herself? I realized that peace at any price was not peace. I went through counseling and participated in a divorce recovery group. I poured out my thoughts, heartaches, and victories in my journal until my fingers hurt.

For years, at least five times a week, I sat at the beach with my journal and cried until my head ached and my eyes were swollen. My mind swirled with questions: Will I ever be strong and stand up for myself? When will I feel free and peaceful? When will I laugh and enjoy life again?

Those old days are a faint memory. Now I go to the beach to have fun, not to cry. I walk on the sand and collect seashells or sit and make sandcastles. I am happy, free, and peaceful. I laugh often and enjoy life far more than I ever thought possible.

One woman told me that after her husband divorced her, she didn't think she could ever be happy again. She cried all the time and felt angry with God for letting the divorce happen. Little by little, she changed from hopeless to hopeful. She now has many friends, travels, and smiles.

Change requires hard work, but it's worth every bit of the struggle. The difficulty comes when you expect too much from yourself. I can remember being impatient and angry with myself when it took me so long to change. My attitude and behavior had been one of fear of my husband and being a people pleaser. The third life lesson is that you can't move from broken to beautiful overnight.

I packaged the nine life lessons in this book to help you move from broken to beautiful. You, too, can change. You can be strong and free one day, laugh again, and enjoy life far more than you ever imagined possible. However, it won't happen within twenty-four hours.

Picture the six- to eight-feet snow banks they get up north. That snow will melt, but not overnight. If it did, it would cause major flooding. Be gentle with yourself. The fairy godmother won't wave a magic wand over you or sprinkle angel dust on you to give you an instantaneous change. So relax and enjoy each step of progress. Celebrate changes, even small ones. Go out to lunch and take a bag of confetti or hats and noisemakers with you. You can celebrate the New Year whenever your new year comes.

In moving from broken to beautiful, not every step will be a step forward, but we'll take a look at that in chapter seven.

Life Lesson Three Activities:
- Journal about the progress you've made to change your life for the better.
- Cut out pictures from a magazine, which depict the changes you're working on, and put them on your vision board.
- Sing or play a song that encourages progress.

Life Lesson Three Affirmations:
- Every day I change for the better.
- I exercise patience with myself.
- I celebrate small steps of progress.

Life Lesson Three Reading and Prayer:

- "Being confident of this, that he who began a good work in you will carry it on to completion until the day of Christ Jesus" (Philippians 1:6).
- "For we are God's handiwork, created in Christ Jesus to do good works, which God prepared in advance for us to do" (Ephesians 2:10).
- "And we all, who with unveiled faces contemplate the Lord's glory, are being transformed into his image with ever-increasing glory, which comes from the Lord, who is the Spirit" (2 Corinthians 3:18).

*Dear God, I see what needs
to change in my life
and want it to happen right away.
I get discouraged when it doesn't,
or when I have a setback.
Help me be hopeful,
yet gentle with myself.
Amen.*

Life Lesson Three Journal

Date: _____

_____

_____

_____

_____

_____

_____

_____

_____

_____

_____

_____

_____

_____

_____

_____

_____

_____

_____

_____

_____

_____

_____

_____

_____

_____

_____

_____

_____

_____

Chapter 4: Admit Your Mistakes

The fourth life lesson in moving from broken to beautiful is to admit your mistakes. One Sunday afternoon, my son wanted to go to an amusement park with a friend. Both boys were thirteen years old at the time. I told my son, "I can drop you off or pick you up. Check with your friend and see if his mother is available to drive one way."

My son called. His friend said he would ask his mother and call right back.
When the phone rang, my son raced to answer it. His father, who usually wasn't home on Sunday afternoons, was there. He grabbed our son under the armpits, lifted him up in the air, and screamed in his face, "When I'm home, I answer the phone."

In the past, either one of us could have answered the phone without the explosion that occurred that day.

The incidents of child abuse had multiplied over the years, and this time my son snapped. He beat up his father. I sat in a corner and thought, *Oh God, let him kill his father. It would be self-defense.* The moment that thought entered my mind, I knew I had stayed too long in a domestic violence marriage. I saw a divorce lawyer. He told me, "Don't say anything to your child or your husband until he is served with divorce papers. We'll have a safety plan in place before that happens."

The following week, my son and I ate dinner at a local restaurant. His eyes welled with tears. "What's wrong?" I asked.

He looked down at his plate and said nothing. I asked again, but my son sat in silence. The third time, I said, "We've always been able to talk in the past. Tell me what's wrong."

He said, "Mom, please get us out of this living hell."

Because of my lawyer's advice not to tell my husband or my son until the divorce papers were served, I said nothing. After the legal separation I told our son, "I'm sorry I stayed in that marriage so long. You paid the price for my mistake. I'm the adult and your mother. As a parent, I should have protected you and never have allowed you to go through all that you did." I wiped the tears gushing down my face and struggled to speak between sobs. "I'm so sorry. I was wrong to stay. I was wrong to pretend everything was okay when it wasn't. The longer I stayed, the worse it got for you."

We both cried. My son forgave me. Life wasn't perfect after my admission, but it improved little by little. I made a conscious effort to be the adult and parent my child needed and deserved.

Years later he told me on the phone, "You did the best you knew how. You were a good mom."

I felt six feet tall, and that's tall for

someone my height.

What have you said or done that hurt your family, friends, or coworkers? When will you call the person on the phone or meet face-to-face to admit your mistakes? Do it for your own good.

If the person you hurt has already passed away, you can write an admission of your mistakes in a letter and read it to a trustworthy friend, a mentor, or your counselor. Take ownership of the mistake so that it loses its hold over you.

Life Lesson Four Activities:
- Journal about the mistakes you've made and how you will admit them to those you hurt.
- Accept the fact that the person may have a positive or a negative response to your admission.
- Afterward, play relaxing music, bake cookies, or go for a walk.

Life Lesson Four Affirmations:
- I admit my mistakes without making excuses for them.
- I apologize for my wrongdoing.
- I make amends to the best of my ability.

Life Lesson Four Reading and Prayer:

- "Whoever conceals their sins does not prosper, but the one who confesses and renounces them finds mercy" (Proverbs 28:13).
- "If we confess our sins, he is faithful and just and will forgive us our sins and purify us from all unrighteousness" (1 John 1:9).
- "So I strive always to keep my conscience clear before God and man" (Acts 24:16).

Dear God, I've made a mess of my life.
I've hurt the ones I love the most.
Help me admit my mistakes
and do better in the future.
Amen.

Life Lesson Four Journal

Date: _____

_____

_____

_____

_____

_____

_____

_____

_____

_____

_____

_____

_____

_____

_____

_____

_____

_____

_____

_____

_____

_____

_____

_____

_____

_____

_____

Chapter 5: Laughter Is Still Good Medicine

The fifth lesson in moving from broken to beautiful is laughter is still good medicine. At Christmastime in 2000, I found a suspicious lump on my left breast. My doctor ordered a mammogram and an ultrasound, and then referred me to a surgeon. Before the surgical biopsy, I feared the surgeon would biopsy the wrong breast. So I wrote, "No, no, no" on the wrong one with a black magic marker and drew an arrow to the one that had the tumor. I wrote, "Yes, yes, yes" on that one and drew a poinsettia on it with red and green magic markers. After all, it was three days before Christmas. Because of the cold surgical room, I wore my Christmas socks. My only regret the day of the biopsy is that I wasn't awake to hear the surgical team laugh at my magic marker masterpiece.

On January 3, 2001, I received a diagnosis of breast cancer. The story keeps getting better. Doesn't it? There's an expression from Friedrich Nietzsche that says, "That which does not kill us makes us stronger." At the time of this writing in 2015, I should be able to bench press a Buick.

My surgeon referred me to a medical

oncologist, a doctor in charge of chemotherapy treatment. Her name was Dr. Fink. Yes, that was her real name. I can't make up things like that.

You should have heard my family laugh when I told them the doctor's name. "Dr. who? Really? Spell that."

I realized I could tremble at the thought of the "Big C," or I could get the endorphins, those natural pain relievers, going in my body. Since laughter produces endorphins, I decided to concentrate on the "Big L—Laughter." I watched one comedy after another. *America's Funniest Home Videos* became one of my favorite TV programs. One evening, I sat alone and laughed so hard during one of the home videos that my sides hurt. I also borrowed, rented, or purchased comedies to watch.

Since I received lots of get-well cards, I asked my family and friends to send me funny cards, jokes, and one-liners. They did, and I set the funny cards on the dining room table and the buffet to laugh at every time I looked at them again.

One day after work, I stopped for a massage. I told David, my massage therapist, "Don't rub my head, because my hair will fall out. He didn't touch my head. After the massage, I stood alone in the room to get ready to leave. I gasped in horror. Hair covered the sheets.

"David," I called. I swallowed hard, pointed to the sheets, and said, "I'm so sorry."

He looked at the sheets, and then at me. He said, "I'm going to have to charge you extra to vacuum the sheets."

I laughed until I cried.

For six and a half weeks, I went Monday through Friday to the hospital for radiation treatments. One of my radiation therapists was George. He made me laugh every time he told me about his childhood adventures. I laughed the hardest when he told me about the time he pretended to be Superman, went through the attic floor, and ended up in the hospital.

During my bout with cancer, I joined two cancer support groups. One group met monthly in a private home for a potluck dinner and fun. The other cancer support group met for a monthly meeting at the hospital and went to a local restaurant for dinner on special occasions, such as Christmastime and Valentine's Day. Except for the turbans some of us wore, other people in the restaurant didn't know we were cancer patients.

One evening we dressed up and went to the Bonefish Grill. We laughed and joked more than the other people in the restaurant. The waiter said, "I've never seen a group have so much fun. Are you celebrating a birthday or something?"

We all laughed, and I said, "It's my two-year anniversary of being cancer-free."

Everyone clapped, and the waiter congratulated me.

Cancer taught me the power of laughter. I don't want to get cancer again, but it gave me an appreciation for the gift of life and the power in my choice to find the humor in it.

When was the last time you laughed? Really laughed until tears rolled down your cheeks or your sides ached? What will you do to ensure you laugh often? Don't wait to feel happy. Choose to do so.

No matter what major illness or crisis you or a loved one faces, I encourage you to laugh often. Laughter is still good medicine.

Life Lesson Five Activities:
- Journal about good laughs you've had in the past.
- Check out a comedy or two from your local library.
- Search the Internet for family friendly jokes and one-liners.

Life Lesson Five Affirmations:
- My supply of endorphins for pain relief never runs out.
- I love to laugh.
- I laugh at least three times a day.

Life Lesson Five Reading and Prayer:

- "Blessed are you who weep now, for you will laugh" (Luke 6:21b).
- "A cheerful heart is good medicine, but a crushed spirit dries up the bones" (Proverbs 17:22).
- "She is clothed with strength and dignity; she can laugh at the days to come" (Proverbs 31:25).

Dear God, my spirit is crushed,
and I'm tired of crying.
Help me to see the humor in life
and to laugh each day.
Amen.

Life Lesson Five Journal

Date: _____

_____

_____

_____

_____

_____

_____

_____

_____

_____

_____

_____

Chapter 6: You Can't Move from Broken to Beautiful Alone

The sixth life lesson is that you can't move from broken to beautiful alone. After the legal separation, I joined a divorce recovery group. At the end of my son's junior year of high school, his father announced he was moving out of state and told our son, "Come with me, and I'll send you to a private school with small classes near my new home. Your mother can't afford to send you to a private school."

My son spent the summer with me and moved out of state to attend that private school. I told the divorce recovery group how I had said good-bye to my son at the train station. As the train pulled out, tears flooded my face. All the way back home, I sobbed. Although the car windows were closed, my gut-wrenching sobs were so loud I was convinced people could hear me on the interstate. It's a wonder the car windows didn't rattle and break.

The men and women in that group had experienced similar partings with their children. They had felt that same kind of pain. They listened with compassion and helped me through it.

I also joined a singles group at my church. Most of us were single again. We took square-dance lessons together and had fun. I whirled my petticoats, met new friends, and didn't feel alone and lonely.

I still remember my first Thanksgiving with the singles group. We chipped in for a turkey and each of us took a side dish. We had each other, and our children played together.

If you're going through a divorce, you might want to join a divorce recovery group in moving from broken to beautiful. If you're a widow, you may want to join GriefShare. Maybe you've lost a child. Consider The Compassionate Friends, a support group for parents who have lost a child, regardless of the age of that child. Perhaps you've suffered through domestic violence or sexual assault. The local shelters offer a free hotline and free support groups. Perhaps you struggle with alcohol, illegal drug abuse, or prescription drug abuse. Alcoholics Anonymous and Narcotics Anonymous provide encouragement, support, and an accountability partner (a sponsor), to help you in moving from broken to beautiful.

As I've already mentioned, I joined a divorce recovery group and a singles group. Later on, I participated in two cancer support groups, GriefShare, and The Compassionate Friends. I belonged to so many groups I would get them mixed up. Let's just say that a good breast joke doesn't fly in a church singles group.

I had a unique prayer warrior support group at the men's prison where I did part of my counseling residency. The night before my cancer surgery, the prisoners prayed for me in the chapel. When I returned after surgery, one of them told me, "Ms. Yvonne, I prayed and fasted for you."

I wonder how many cancer patients receive a get-well card signed by prisoners and correctional officers. I still have the card they signed.

No matter what you're going through, there's a group to help you. There's probably a group for people who don't have a specific problem. They call it the "Waiting for the Other Shoe to Drop" group.

Life Lesson Six Activities:

- Search on the Internet for a group to meet your specific needs.
- If you're an introvert, ask an extroverted friend to attend the first one or two group meetings with you.
- If no group meets in your area, find one that meets online or confide in a mentor, a trusted friend, or a counselor.

Life Lesson Six Affirmations:

- I attend a group to meet my specific needs.
- I share my burdens with those who understand me.
- I receive the support and encouragement I need.

Life Lesson Six Reading and Prayer:

- "Two are better than one, because they have a good return for their labor: If either of them falls down, one can help the other up. But pity anyone who falls and has no one to help them up" (Ecclesiastes 4:9–10).
- "Finally, all of you, be like-minded, be sympathetic, love one another, be compassionate and humble" (1 Peter 3:8).
- "Therefore encourage one another and build each other up, just as in fact you are doing" (1 Thessalonians 5:11).

Dear God, you know my heartaches and struggles.
Lead me to the right group or person who can listen with compassion.
Amen.

Life Lesson Six Journal

Date: _____

_____

_____

_____

_____

_____

_____

_____

_____

_____

_____

_____

_____

_____

_____

_____

_____

_____

_____

_____

_____

_____

_____

_____

_____

_____

_____

_____

Chapter 7: A Setback Doesn't Mean Failure

The seventh life lesson in moving from broken to beautiful is that a setback doesn't mean failure. We can take our recovery too seriously at times and be our own worst enemy. When I experienced a setback, in my mind it was failure—total and complete failure.

After the legal separation, I never wanted to say anything against my estranged husband in the presence of our son. After all, my husband was still his father. One day, my son came home after spending time with his dad. "Dad bought me a stereo set, Mom. It cost a lot of money, and he said you have to give him half of the child support back for this month to help him pay for it."

So much for my good intentions not to say anything against his father in front of my son. I let my tongue rip loose until I saw the hurt look on his face. I stopped immediately. No matter what, my husband was still his father. My son needed both of us, and I learned to keep my mouth shut—not an easy lesson for a woman who likes to talk and hear herself think out loud. I didn't see that incident as one poor choice. Instead I saw it as a failure. My single parent friends helped me distinguish between the two. My life wasn't over. I could still get back up and move forward.

I learned another lesson about a setback during my bout with cancer. I did well after my first chemotherapy treatment, and my surgeon told me my white blood cell counts looked great. I decided I didn't need those Neupogen shots after my second chemotherapy treatment to stimulate the blood system to make white blood cells. I could fight infections on my own.

I didn't have an ounce of medical training, and I didn't have an ounce of common sense either. Within a few days, I felt tired and weak. I called my cancer support group mentor and said, "Dawn, I can hardly walk. My left cheek and jaw are swollen, and the mouth sores are worse."

"Yvonne, go to the ER to be checked."

A few hours later, I was a patient in the hospital with a low blood count of five hundred. Normal is between four thousand and eleven thousand. I ended up with Neutropenia, a blood condition in which the immune system is dangerously low. I also had an infected parotid (salivary) gland. I spent a week in the hospital in isolation—torture for an extrovert like me.

In my mind, that setback was failure— total and complete failure. Since my bachelor's degree was in Spanish and English and my second master's degree in counseling, I could scold myself in either language, and then counsel my sagging spirit.

I didn't give up because of that setback. I

asked the nurse for paper and pencil and wrote what later became chapters in my book, *Finding Hope for Your Journey through Breast Cancer*.

My poor choice was a setback, but it didn't mean total failure. I learned the hard way to take those shots for the rest of my chemotherapy treatments. That setback occurred fourteen years ago, and I thank God I'm still here.

You won't get it right every time either. Sometimes you'll make mistakes. When that happens, I encourage you not to see your setback as a failure. The only failure is to let a setback cause you to give up.

Life Lesson Seven Activities:
- Journal about good choices you've made in your life.
- Talk to a friend about a lesson you learned from a mistake.
- Go to breakfast or lunch with a friend to celebrate not giving up after a setback.

Life Lesson Seven Affirmations:
- I'm a human being with strengths and weaknesses.
- I do the best I can.
- I learn from my mistakes.

Life Lesson Seven Reading and Prayer:

- "Brothers and sisters, I do not consider myself yet to have taken hold of it. But one thing I do: Forgetting what is behind and straining toward what is ahead, I press on toward the goal to win the prize" (Philippians 3:13–14a).
- "Though he may stumble, he will not fall, for the LORD upholds him with his hand" (Psalm 37:24).
- "Let us not become weary in doing good, for at the proper time we will reap a harvest if we do not give up" (Galatians 6:9).

*Dear God, sometimes I say
or do foolish things.
Help me not to beat myself up
because I'm not perfect.
I ask you for the strength to get back up
and continue moving forward.
Amen.*

Life Lesson Seven Journal

Date: _____

Chapter 8: Nurture Your Body and Spirit

The eighth life lesson in moving from broken to beautiful is to nurture your body and spirit. As women, we make great caregivers for others. We nurture everyone else but ourselves.

As I mentioned earlier, I survived cancer. When I received my diagnosis, I called my friend to tell her. "Nancy, I have breast cancer."

"Yvonne, you've got to see Dr. Sharon. She's a doctor of naturopathy and uses a holistic approach. She'll help you."

I agreed to go with Nancy to Dr. Sharon's office. Dr. Sharon is a tall brunette. I walked into her office, looked up at her, and said, "Dr. Sharon, how long is this going to take? I'm really busy today. I have to help my neighbor's daughter, and other people are depending on me too."

She said, "Yvonne, do you want to live?"

"Of course I want to live. I just don't want to lose my hair, eyebrows, and eyelashes."

"What quality of life do you want to have?"

"A good one, Dr. Sharon."

"You have to take responsibility for your life and take care of your body."

She said, "No red meat."

I said, "No problem."

She said, "No pork."

I said, "No problem."

She said, "No Dairy Queen ice cream."

I said, "Problem."

"Once in a while, I like to have a Dairy Queen Hawaiian Blizzard. It has pineapple, bananas, and coconut. Fruit has nutritional value."

She ignored my justification for eating Dairy Queen ice cream.

However, Dr. Sharon also told me, "You have to exercise even if it is just a short walk each day in your neighborhood."

I went through chemotherapy and thirty-three rounds of radiation. After the last radiation treatment, I did have a Dairy Queen Hawaiian Blizzard, and it wasn't the mini size. We all understood it was time for a treat.

A year later, I got my hair back. I got my eyebrows and eyelashes back. I got my life back. Dr. Sharon was right. I had to take responsibility for my life and take care of my body. I started eating better. I don't eat red meat. I don't eat pork, but I'm not perfect. Every so often I eat a Dairy Queen Hawaiian Blizzard.

Exercise is part of my life. Whether it is aqua aerobics, a brisk walk outside, or low-impact aerobics with a DVD at home, I exercise almost daily. In addition to my desk and desktop computer, I have a stand-up computer table and a laptop. I don't want to sit for hours and end up with "a computer spread." I often set the timer for every thirty minutes to an hour. When the timer goes off, I walk around the house a few times.

When I travel, I take workout clothes and a bathing suit and look for a gym or a swimming pool. I want to keep my body healthy and mobile.

Unfortunately, there aren't department stores or boutiques where you can trade your body in for a new model. What will you do to take care of your body? What commitment will you make to eat right and to exercise?

Now let's look at care of our spirit. Five years ago, I lost two aunts, my mother, and my only child, my precious son. Part of me wanted to die and be with them. The other part of me fought to go on. They all would want me to do that.

In my quiet time, I remembered a conversation I had with my son before he passed away. He said, "Mom, you need a cell phone. Everyone has a cell phone."

"Not everyone. I don't."

"Mom, that's why I call you B.C.—Before Christ."

I nurtured my grieving spirit and bought the latest smartphone. I planned to go to my son's Celebration of Life service with that Android smartphone and at least know how to make and receive calls and utilize email on it.

Before my son's Celebration of Life service, I walked up to his open casket and whispered in his ear, "Honey, I bought a cell phone in your memory." I held the Android in my hand. He couldn't hear me or see that cell phone, but it nurtured my spirit to do it anyway.

One of his friends mentioned my son had

an iPhone when he was alive. When my contract expired on the Android, I switched to an iPhone in his memory.

Another way I nurture my spirit is to walk at the beach and listen to the waves. In January of 2015, I left cold weather and an ice storm in Virginia and attended a speakers' boot camp in Florida. At lunchtime I ate without conversing much with the other speakers in order to take advantage of the warmer weather and walk on the beach. At the end of each day, I raced out the door again to walk on the beach until sunset. On my last day in Florida, I recorded the sound of the ocean waves. I played that recording after my return home when the snowstorms kept me inside.

When will you nurture your body and spirit? How will you do it? Picture one thing you can do to start the process.

Life Lesson Eight Activities:
- Prepare a meal with a variety of fresh fruit and vegetables.
- Walk, swim, or choose another form of exercise you like this week.
- Light a scented candle and play easy listening music as you relax.

Life Lesson Eight Affirmations:
- I exercise at least five times weekly.
- I eat healthy foods most of the time.
- I take time to relax each day.

Life Lesson Eight Reading and Prayer:

- "For the entire law is fulfilled in keeping this one command: 'Love your neighbor **as yourself**'" (Galatians 5:14, emphasis mine).
- "'I have the right to do anything,' you say—but not everything is beneficial. 'I have the right to do anything'—but I will not be mastered by anything" (1 Corinthians 6:12).
- "Above all else, guard your heart, for everything you do flows from it" (Proverbs 4:23).

Dear God, I find it easier to take care of others
and forget about taking care of me.
Help me love myself enough
to nurture my body and spirit.
Amen.

Life Lesson Eight Journal

Date: _____

_____

_____

_____

_____

_____

_____

_____

_____

_____

_____

_____

_____

_____

_____

Chapter 9: Help Someone Else Move from Broken to Beautiful

The ninth life lesson is to help someone else move from broken to beautiful. We can take our pain and turn it into good by helping others through theirs.

As a church lay counselor, I facilitated a support group for women. As I approached the end of the twelve weeks, the women wanted to know what book we would use next. I realized I had moved from broken to beautiful because I could help them without harm to my own self-care. I returned to college for my second master's degree. This time it was in counseling.

My first counseling job was in a men's prison. Several of the inmates in the substance abuse program were moving from broken to beautiful when they no longer felt sorry for themselves. They didn't blame the judge, their lawyer, their family and friends anymore, and they wanted to help me.

Two of them carpeted my office. On my birthday, two other inmates in the program showed up with a wooden stool they made for me with the help of a prisoner outside of the program. Engraved on it were the words, "Ms. Yvonne." On my one-year anniversary of working there, other men in the substance abuse treatment group surprised me. They gave me a new wooden sign to hang over my office door with our program name, "Moving Forward," engraved on it. Other guys in the program made a wooden bookcase to store my books. Still others managed to get me a shiny corner desk with a computer station. We won't ask about the details on how they obtained it, but they did it legitimately.

One afternoon, "Sticky Fingers," who struggled to stay out of people's lockers, said, "Ms. Yvonne, I won't be able to finish college if I don't pass my Spanish class. I don't get the grammar."

"Go get your book, and let's take a look at it together."

With a little help from me, Sticky Fingers passed his Spanish class. He was so grateful he promised to landscape my yard when he was released from prison. "Whatever you want, Ms. Yvonne, I'll do it."

I thanked him for the offer but told him that wouldn't be necessary. For ethical reasons, I couldn't accept free work from any client.

Not only did the guys help me, they also helped each other. "Snake" needed help in math to pass the GED, and "Blade" offered to help him. We celebrated when Snake passed the math section. "Tunnel" couldn't read past a first-grade level, but "Snitch" helped him until his release. At that time, Tunnel tested at an eighth-grade level. We were so proud of his progress.

Months after the progress Snake and Tunnel made, I was riding with Sally in her car on our return from a road trip. We took the wrong exit and ended up, of all places, in a neighborhood where drugs abounded. That was the one place Tunnel told me, "Never, ever, under any circumstances go there." But there we were.

Sally rushed to find a place to turn around and get back on the interstate. She mumbled something about a vision of two women found in a local dumpster clutching their mace and the latest copy of a Bible study workbook. I think she watches too many episodes of *Law and Order*. She frantically focused on getting out of there, but I focused on one thought, my former client, Martin. "Dear God, please let me see Martin."

I opened my eyes, and there he was. "Stop the car and pray," I yelled. In my Capri pants with the yellow flowers on the hem and the matching cardigan, I darted out of the car and into the streets of that area.

Martin was crossing the street and heading straight for me. The skinny boy, with a chain on his belt, beside him froze.

"Ms. Yvonne, I'm not doing well." Martin's shoulders slumped.

I almost didn't recognize him. He had lost weight. He had circles under his eyes and a new scar on his face. More than that, he looked like six feet seven inches of walking despair.

Somehow I sensed this was my last chance to reach him. I grabbed his hands. The skinny boy darted off into the shadows like a rat running from the light. I said, "I know. That's why you're here, Martin, and not at home in your neighborhood."

He nodded, but said nothing.

"Martin, God loves you, and he has a future and a hope for you. I love you too. Now go home. You don't belong here."

I hugged him and walked away wondering if I'd ever see him again.

About two months later, an inmate stopped by my office and said, "I heard through the prison pipeline that Martin is in jail."

The mama bear in me came out. One of my cubs was in jail again. He had graduated from the program. He was out there and had a good job. He had been doing well. I went to the jail to see him and told the clerk at the desk, "Don't tell him who his visitor is."

I had my jail-based counselor badge on, so the clerk listened to me.

Martin looked startled when he saw me. The glass separated us, and we both reached for the jail phones in order to talk to each other. He looked better. His face was fuller and his shoulders straighter.

I said, "Hi, Martin."

"Ms. Yvonne."

"What happened?" I asked.

"Something I did before I went home. I'm here until my court date and sentencing."

"One of the guys told me you were here."

"I'm glad you came. I wanted you to know

I'm clean and sober. I've been clean and sober for a while. The day you told me to go home I did. I'm here, but it's different now. I have a purpose. I'm a new man with a new life, and I wanted you to know that." He put his hand up to the glass, and I put my hand up to meet his.

"Thank you, Ms. Yvonne," he whispered. "You saved my life. I'm here, but I'm not here. Inside, I'm free."

I realized in that moment, others might have seen a different picture. They would have shaken their heads and seen a man in jail guilty of a crime for which he deserved to be punished. They would have seen another wasted life, a story of how society had wronged him, or how he had wronged society. They would have seen a man destined to rot in jail for the rest of his life. They would have seen a broken man.

That's not what I saw. I saw a glimmer of hope. The hope that says there's a new beginning. Whether it's this side of the glass or that side of the glass, it's still a new life. He has moved from broken to beautiful even behind bars and can help those incarcerated with him to do the same.

Your pain and suffering don't have to be in vain either. Wherever you are, you, too, can move from broken to beautiful. What goal or dream do you have? Do you feel a nudge to return to college, to enroll in computer classes, or to enhance your job skills? Look into it. Right now, it may seem impossible to reach that goal. When the time is right, you will. One day you, too, will give back what was given to you. You will help others move from broken to beautiful. When you reach that place in your life, you will have moved from broken to beautiful and beyond.

Life Lesson Nine Activities:
- Journal about what it would mean to you to help someone else move from broken to beautiful.
- Draw a picture of how you can help someone move forward.
- Encourage a friend going through a trial.

Life Lesson Nine Affirmations:
- I have moved from broken to beautiful.
- I give back what was once given to me.
- I help others move from broken to beautiful.

Life Lesson Nine Reading and Prayer:

- "Carry each other's burdens, and in this way you will fulfill the law of Christ" (Galatians 6:2).
- "Each of us should please our neighbors for their good, to build them up" (Romans 15:2).
- "In everything I did, I showed you that by this kind of hard work we must help the weak, remembering the words the Lord Jesus himself said: 'It is more blessed to give than to receive'" (Acts 20:35).

Dear God, thank you for all those
who helped me
move from broken to beautiful.
Now it's my turn.
Show me the people
you want me to encourage and support
so they, too, can
move from broken to beautiful.
Amen.

Life Lesson Nine Journal

Date: _____

_____

_____

_____

_____

_____

_____

_____

_____

_____

_____

_____

_____

_____

Appendix A: Additional Affirmations

- I refuse to be stuck in the past.
- My past will not determine my future.
- I am victorious.
- I enjoy making each day better than the one before.
- I don't cower before a bully.
- I see through the lies and threats of a bully.
- I set healthy boundaries with a bully.
- I aim for progress, not perfection.
- I treat myself with gentleness.
- I understand that change takes time.
- I make mistakes, but I'm not a mistake.
- I'm not perfect, and that's okay.
- I don't blame others for my mistakes.
- I see the funny side of my experiences.
- I read jokes and one-liners often.
- I watch comedies three or four times a week.
- I choose to laugh daily.
- I accept help from trustworthy friends.
- I meet with an accountability partner weekly in person or on the phone.
- I learn from those who have endured similar struggles.
- I will not give up.
- I get back up when I fall down.
- I use a setback as a lesson in growth.

- I limit my intake of sugar.
- I exercise regularly, regardless of the weather.
- I meditate and journal each day.
- I sleep seven or eight hours each night.
- I support those on the journey from broken to beautiful.
- I empathize with others in their struggle to move forward.
- I help others celebrate their progress.

Appendix B: Additional Readings

Life Lesson 1: You Can't Change the Past

- "He reached down from on high and took hold of me; he drew me out of deep waters" (Psalm 18:16).
- "He rescued me from my powerful enemy, from my foes, who were too strong for me" (Psalm 18:17).
- "He lifted me out of the slimy pit, out of the mud and mire; he set my feet on a rock and gave me a firm place to stand" (Psalm 40:2).
- "For with you is the fountain of life; in your light we see light" (Psalm 36:9).

Life Lesson 2: A Bully Can't Beat You in Your Life Journey

- "But he said to me, 'My grace is sufficient for you, for my power is made perfect in weakness.' Therefore I will boast all the more gladly about my weaknesses, so that Christ's power may rest on me" (2 Corinthians 12:9).
- "I thank and praise you, God of my ancestors: You have given me wisdom and power" (Daniel 2:23a).
- "So do not fear, for I am with you; do not be dismayed, for I am your God. I will strengthen you and help you; I will uphold

you with my righteous right hand" (Isaiah 41:10).
- "And God is able to bless you abundantly, so that in all things at all times, having all that you need, you will abound in every good work" (2 Corinthians 9:8).

Life Lesson 3: You Can't Move from Broken to Beautiful Overnight
- "But do not forget this one thing, dear friends: With the Lord a day is like a thousand years, and a thousand years are like a day" (2 Peter 3:8).
- "Better a patient person than a warrior, one with self-control than one who takes a city" (Proverbs 16:32).
- "Be patient, then, brothers and sisters, until the Lord's coming. See how the farmer waits for the land to yield its valuable crop, patiently waiting for the autumn and spring rains. You too, be patient and stand firm, because the Lord's coming is near" (James 5:7–8).

Life Lesson 4: Admit Your Mistakes
- "Let us draw near to God with a sincere heart and with the full assurance that faith brings, having our hearts sprinkled to cleanse us from a guilty conscience and having our bodies washed with pure water" (Hebrews 10:22).

- "If we say that we have no sin, we are deceiving ourselves and the truth is not in us" (1 John 1:8).
- "When I kept silent, my bones wasted away through my groaning all day long. For day and night your hand was heavy on me; my strength was sapped as in the heat of summer" (Psalm 32:3–4).
- "Then I acknowledged my sin to you and did not cover up my iniquity. I said, 'I will confess my transgressions to the Lord.' And you forgave the guilt of my sin" (Psalm 32:5).

Life Lesson 5: Laughter Is Still Good Medicine

- "A happy heart makes the face cheerful" (Proverbs 15:13).
- "A time to weep and a time to laugh, a time to mourn and a time to dance" (Ecclesiastes 3:4).
- "But the cheerful heart has a continual feast" (Proverbs 15:15b).

Life Lesson 6: You Can't Move from Broken to Beautiful Alone

- "Walk with the wise and become wise" (Proverbs 13:20).
- "Thus you will walk in the ways of the good and keep to the paths of the righteous" (Proverbs 2:20).

- "As iron sharpens iron, so one person sharpens another" (Proverbs 27:17).

Life Lesson 7: A Setback Doesn't Mean Failure

- "My flesh and my heart may fail, but God is the strength of my heart and my portion forever" (Psalm 73:26).
- "Therefore, since we are surrounded by such a great cloud of witnesses, let us throw off everything that hinders and the sin that so easily entangles. And let us run with perseverance the race marked out for us" (Hebrews 12:1).
- "Let your eyes look straight ahead; fix your gaze directly before you" (Proverbs 4:25).

Life Lesson 8: Nurture Your Body and Spirit

- "Dear friend, I pray that you may enjoy good health and that all may go well with you, even as your soul is getting along well" (3 John 1:2).
- "In vain you rise early and stay up late, toiling for food to eat—for he grants sleep to those he loves" (Psalm 127:2).
- "Do you not know that your bodies are temples of the Holy Spirit, who is in you, whom you have received from God?" (1 Corinthians 6:19).

Life Lesson 9: Help Someone Else Move from Broken to Beautiful

- "Be completely humble and gentle; be patient, bearing with one another in love" (Ephesians 4:2).
- "And let us consider how we may spur one another on toward love and good deeds" (Hebrews 10:24).
- "Do not let any unwholesome talk come out of your mouths, but only what is helpful for building others up according to their needs, that it may benefit those who listen" (Ephesians 4:29).

Appendix C: Resources

Cancer Links

www.cancer.org
American Cancer Society information for patients, family, friends, survivors, professionals, donors, and volunteers; bookstore and gift shop, cancer facts and figures, research program, stories of hope, Relay For Life, international program.

www.thebreastcancersite.greatergood.com
Shop the extensive pink ribbon selection and help fund mammograms for women in need.

www.cleaningforareason.org
Find free professional housecleaning and maid service for women undergoing treatment for any kind of cancer.

www.asbestos.com
Find the latest information on asbestos, mesothelioma, and other cancers caused by asbestos. Free support books and veterans assistance also available.

www.nationalbreastcancer.org
The National Breast Cancer Foundation, Inc. spreads knowledge and offers hope in the fight against breast cancer. It also funds free mammograms for women who can't afford them.

Divorce Recovery Support Group Links

www.divorcecare.org
Divorce Care is a divorce recovery support group that offers hope and healing for those going through separation and divorce.

www.freshstartdivorcerecovery.wordpress.com
Fresh Start offers teaching and support for those dealing with divorce.

You can also call local counseling agencies, the Department of Social Services, your local Community Services Board, the nearest YMCA, or your minister, priest, or rabbi to find a divorce support group.

Domestic Violence Links

www.dvalianza.org
The National Latino Alliance for the Elimination of Domestic Violence (Alianza) addresses the needs of Latino/a families and communities in community education, policy advocacy, research, and training and technical assistance.

www.idvaac.org
The Institute on Domestic Violence in the African American Community (IDVAAC) is an organization that focuses on the unique circumstances of African Americans as they face issues related to domestic violence.

www.faithtrustinstitute.org
The Faith Trust Institute is a national, multifaith, multicultural training and education organization with global reach working to end sexual and domestic violence.

www.ncadv.org
The National Coalition Against Domestic Violence offers Fact Sheets and a State Coalition List. It works to empower battered women and children, to promote and unify direct service programs, and to educate and alert the public.

www.thehotline.org
The National Domestic Violence Hotline provides help for families, friends, and survivors of domestic violence. Services for the deaf and a blog are available.

www.theraveproject.org
Rave is an initiative that seeks to bring knowledge and social action together to assist families of faith impacted by abuse. It offers resources for women, the clergy, and the community.

Grief Recovery Support Group Links

www.compassionatefriends.org
The Compassionate Friends offers grief support to those who have lost a child or grandchild. It helps them find support, understanding, and healing.

www.griefshare.org
GriefShare offers help and healing to those who have lost a loved one.

Substance Use Recovery Links

www.alcoholics-anonymous.org
The official Alcoholics Anonymous site, how to find an AA meeting, information about AA, services for members, media resources, AA archives.

www.alcoholicsanonymous.com
The Alcoholics Resource Center is an unofficial website for AA members. It provides information and social networking to support AA members.

www.christians-in-recovery.org
Christians in Recovery (CIR) offers more than three thousand pages of information and resources for recovery from abuse, family dysfunction, depression, anxiety, grief, relationships, and addictions of alcohol, drugs, food, pornography, sexual addiction, and more.

www.na.org
The Narcotics Anonymous site, NA meeting search, regional and area links, facts about NA, information for professionals, networking online with professionals, NA events, news, books and booklets in thirty-two languages.

www.celebraterecovery.com
Celebrate Recovery is a Christian recovery program that helps thousands of people recover from alcoholism and many other addictions. A person may attend with a desire to work the steps for healing with any number of "hurts, hang-ups, or habits" (compulsive behaviors).

*All links were in working order at the time of publication.

About the Author

Yvonne Ortega is a Licensed Professional Counselor, a Licensed Substance Abuse Treatment Practitioner, and a Clinically Certified Domestic Violence Counselor. She is the author of *Finding Hope for Your Journey through Breast Cancer* (Revell) and a contributing author to *The Embrace of a Father* (Bethany House) and *Transformed* (Wine Press). She has presented writers' workshops from coast to coast in the USA. Yvonne received a literary award at the Maine Fellowship of Christian Writers in 2002. She also received the Persistence Award at the American Christian Writers Conference in Virginia in 2002 for continuing to write during the time of aggressive treatment for cancer. As a survivor of domestic violence, breast cancer, and the loss of her only child, she loves to speak to audiences in either English or Spanish about her journey in moving from broken to beautiful. Yvonne regularly conducts compelling, uplifting, interactive keynotes, workshops, seminars, and retreats for women who wear anything from designer suits to jumpsuits. She can be reached at **www.yvonneortega.com** and loves to connect with her readers through her website blog and through email at **yvonne@yvonneortega.com**.

Yvonne has spoken in English for such organizations as cancer support groups, churches, Kairos Prison Ministry, the Peninsula Women's Network, NSA (National Speakers Association) Virginia Pro Track Speakers Academy, Stonecroft Ministries, the Virginia Breast Cancer Foundation Peninsula Chapter, and Women of Value in Every Nation in Richmond, Virginia. She has spoken in Spanish in New Jersey for Stonecroft Ministries and at a Spanish retreat for Olive Grove Church in Nuevo, CA.

Connect with

Yvonne Ortega

Facebook: Yvonne Ortega
Twitter: Yvonne Ortega1
LinkedIn: Yvonne Ortega

Visit
www.yvonneortega.com
to book Yvonne to speak at
your next event.